Tugboats

Holt, Rinehart and Winston / New York

Richard Rosenblum
TUGBOATS

Copyright © 1976 by Richard Rosenblum
All rights reserved, including the right to reproduce
this book or portions thereof in any form.
Published simultaneously in Canada by Holt, Rinehart
and Winston of Canada, Limited.
Printed in the United States of America
First Edition

Library of Congress Cataloging in Publication Data

Rosenblum, Richard.
   Tugboats.

  SUMMARY: Traces the history of tugboats, how
they are built, and their various uses.
   1. Tugboats—Juvenile literature. [1. Tugboats]
I. Title.
VM464.R67   623.82'32   75-28055
ISBN 0-03-015311-5

To Barbara

The Early Craft

Before the steam engine was invented, great sailing ships carried passengers and cargo from one end of the world to the other. When a ship arrived at a harbor, oarsmen helped pull her into her dock. When she was ready to sail out again, she was pulled out into the harbor, where her sails would catch the wind and send her on her way.

In 1765 James Watt invented the steam engine. Other engineers made other contributions to the idea of a steam-powered vessel. Soon no longer would manpower be needed. In 1802 an engine was added to the rowboat—and the first tug was born. The *Charlotte Dundas*, built in England, was put to work towing barges on canals.

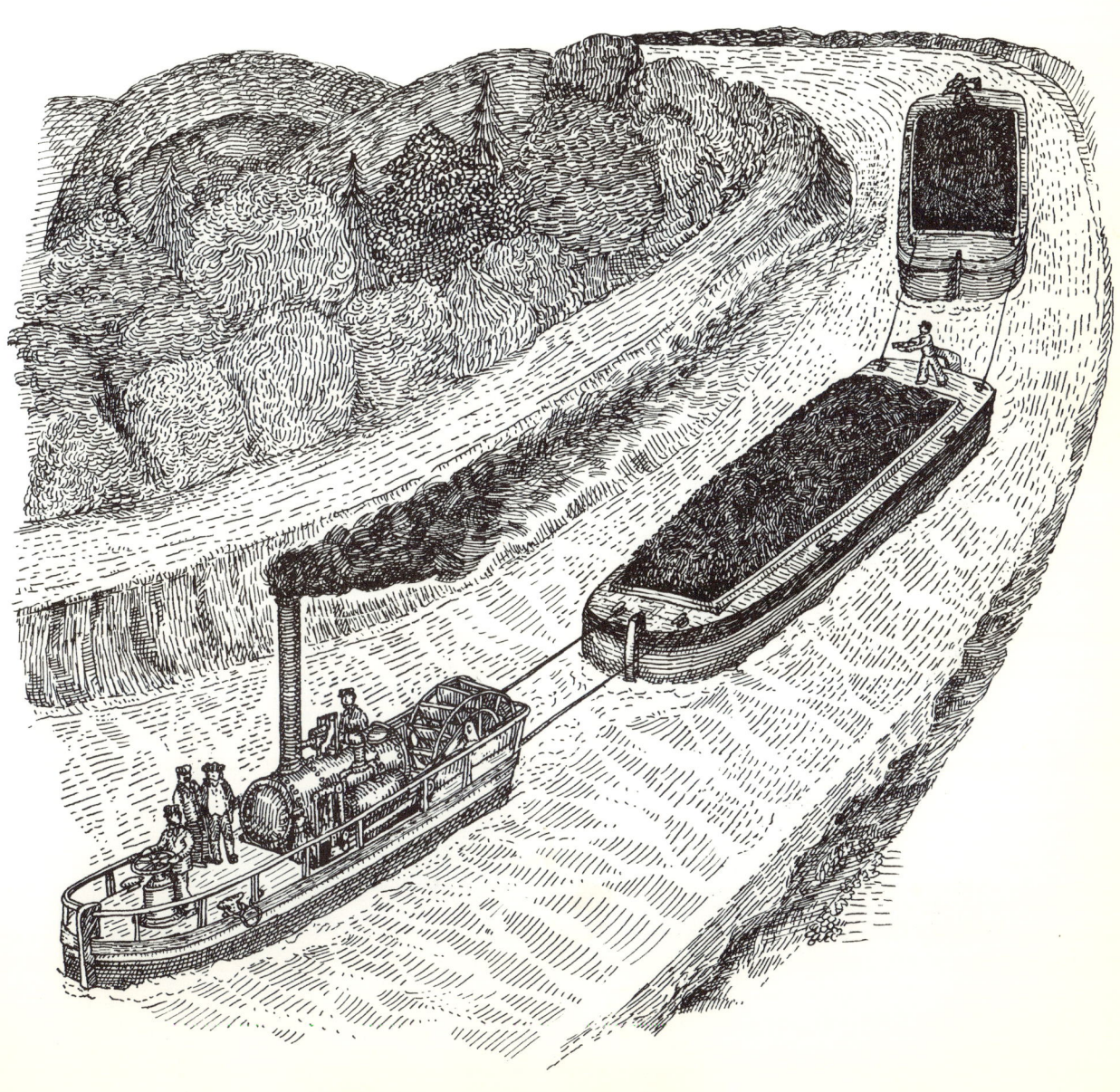

Puffing giant clouds of smoke from the wood and coal they burned as fuel, the first steamboats took over the task of helping the sailing ships in and out of harbors.

Sailing ships were replaced by giant ships with steam engines, and by the 1900's such great steamships as the *Titanic, Leviathan, Majestic, Aquitania, Rex, Normandie* and *Queen Mary* were arriving in our harbors from all over the world.

Ports and Harbors

Today brightly colored tugboats are a common sight in the ports and harbors of the world. Tooting their whistles, these workhorses of the harbor perform many chores.

Small but powerful, they are easily recognized by their snubby bow, single smokestack, and prominent pilothouse.

Versatile, they both push and pull. They help giant ships squeeze into and out of small docking areas and transport barges, scows, derricks, and cranes.

Inland Rivers

The towboat, a very close relative of the tug, is as familiar a sight on our inland waterways as the tug is in our harbors.

It looks different and performs somewhat differently from the harbor tugs. Rectangular in shape and shallow drafted for plying shallow waters, it has several decks, with machinery, living quarters, and pilot house, each occuping a deck of its own.

The forerunner of the towboat was the cargo-carrying raft floated down the Mississippi to New Orleans, where the cargo was sold and the raft broken up and sold for lumber.

These helpless rafts were replaced by keelboats, more traditional-looking craft, capable of being poled or sailed back up the river with cargo.

With steam the Mississippi steamboat came about. It carried passengers and cargo and sometimes barges tied to its side.

Towboats can be big or small. Unlike the busy workhorse of the harbors, towboats only push.

The pilot or captain watches from the pilot house.

The most powerful towboats push as many as twenty or thirty barges filled with every kind of cargo.

Canal Tugs

Canal tugs are still different.

    Before the invention of steam, canal barges were pulled by any method found handy. Horses, mules, sometimes even men walked along the towpath pulling them along.

    Now tugs are designed expressly for canals. They are built low, with short stacks and a low silhouette, to enable them to pass under bridges.

Ocean-going Tugs

While harbor tugs are capable of going to sea, ocean-going tugs are built expressly for life at sea. Big and powerful, they have special equipment, such as winches, for long tows.

Ocean-going tugs may be at sea for weeks or months at a time pulling a floating dry dock or an off shore oil drilling rig to its destination or towing a distinguished old battleship to some break-up yard across the ocean. A tow from San Francisco to Yokohama that returns to home port by way of Australia is not unusual.

While stationed in exotic ports around the world, ocean-going tugs respond to emergencies at sea. An S.O.S. from a ship in need of help brings tugs racing from all parts of the world. Tugs compete vigorously for salvage and rescue work.

The Annie Eagle—A Tug Is Born

All tugboats painted in one set of colors and carrying the same insignia on their smokestacks belong to one company—the Eagle Tugboat Company. They all fly the company flag.

Company officials decide one day to add a new tugboat to their fleet. Owners, engineers, captain, and naval architects meet to decide how it should be outfitted. They decide the new tug should be a general purpose tug, capable of harbor duty and some ocean towing. They name it *Annie Eagle*.

    A ship yard is contracted to build the new tug.

Once the hull has been built, the main engine installed, and the deck house and pilot house structures are up, the tug is ready for launching.

At her launching she is christened by Anne, for whom she has been named.

Annie Eagle is tried and tested. When the builders and owners are satisfied with her performance, she is turned over to a captain and crew. They sail her on her maiden voyage to her new home in the harbor.

The *Annie Eagle* receives the same welcome as any luxury liner making a maiden voyage. She is greeted by fireboats spraying water into the air. Other ships in the harbor blow their horns and toot their whistles as she is escorted to her berth.

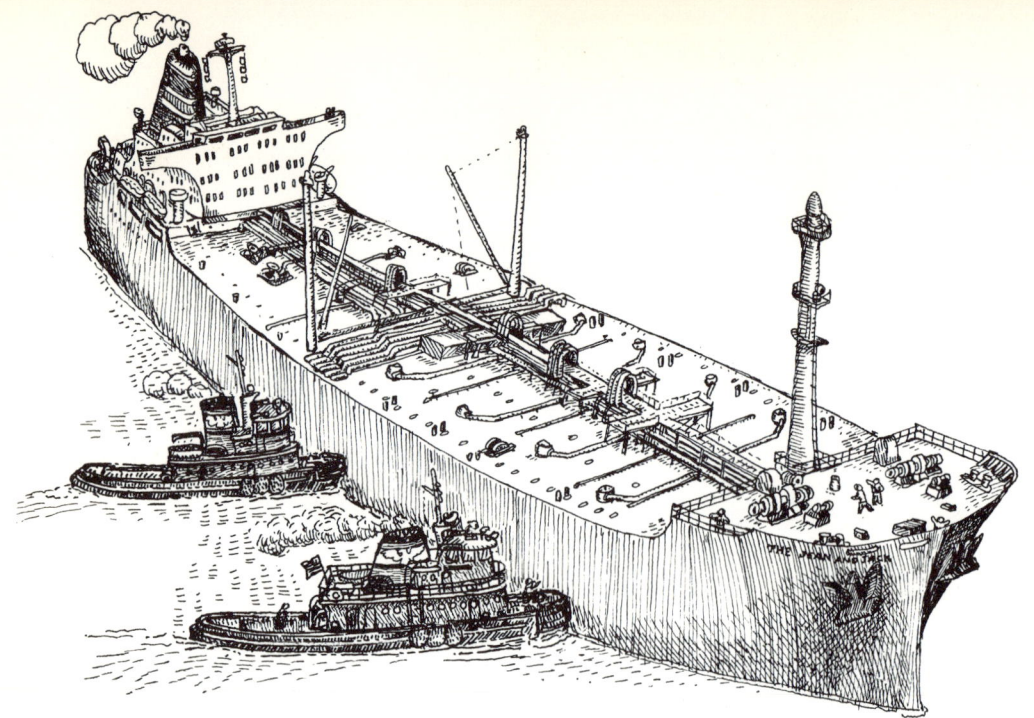

Annie Eagle's first assignment is to help her sistership, *Barbara Eagle*. Together they dock a supertanker arriving from Asia with a load of oil.

Annie Eagle has begun her harbor career. For a long time to come, she will push and pull barges, lighters and scows and will work with floating derricks and cranes.

She will greet one of the magnificent, fully rigged, three-masted sailing and training ships still operating in some parts of the world today.

She will perform in emergencies, helping to fight a fire in the harbor or to break a passage through the ice in winter.

The *Annie's* captain sits at the controls in the pilothouse, which is equipped with a wheel, control console, binnacle, radar, sonar, radio telephone and, of course, a whistle.

The chief engineer and his assistant keep the *Annie's* engines in good working order.

Heaving and securing lines, deckhands keep the ship clean and polished and the equipment in shape.

Some people think the cook is the most important member of the crew.

Tugboats almost always have at least two crews on board at all times, each working a six hour shift.

Colorful tugboats, old and new, are part of the work scene of every harbor and river in the world. They arouse warm, friendly feelings on the part of the sailors who man them and the many people who come to watch them, puffing and tooting along.

About the Author

Richard Rosenblum, a native Brooklynite, lives in Brooklyn Heights with his wife, Barbara, and daughter, Anne. From his windows which overlook the harbor, he lovingly watches every bit of activity that goes on.

   A graduate of Cooper Union, he has free-lanced for many years, illustrating books and magazine articles, designing animated films and doing advertising art. He teaches illustration at Parsons.